My Country

LYNN HARD

With drawings by Garry Shead

ETT IMPRINT

Exile Bay

This edition published as a trade edition of *The Emperor's Tailor*
with the addition of 3 new poems, by ETT Imprint, Exile Bay 2025

ETT IMPRINT
PO Box R1906

Royal Exchange NSW 1225
Australia

First published by ETT Imprint in a limited edition of 50 in 2025

ISBN 978-1-923527-08-9

Cover by Garry Shead

Design by Tom Thompson

This is for Garry Shead and Tom Thompson,
friends and partners in making things up.
Lynn

Other books by Lynn Hard

Dancing on the Drainboard (1992)
Australia Suite (1998)
The Unused Portion (2013)
Poems New & Neglected (2016)
Affection (2021)
The Emporer's Tailor (2025)

Contents

My Country

My country
started with a war
about who would run our lives,
the king and all his distant relatives
or us.
Us won.

It also disentangled church from state,
implicitly saying that items of state were real
and religion a personal delusion
and mixing the real with lies creates fraud.

Also,
there was the matter of
all men being created equal.

My country
had another war
that determined
that adherence to that tenet
was not to be selective.

And my country,
somewhat slower than others,
eventually
noticed women
as equal citizens.

Over time
other omissions and wrongs
were made right.

Other wars were fought
because
all of the above
would not let us
accept that a larger number of bayonets
excused the elimination
of life, liberty and the pursuit of happiness
for anyone.

I agree with all of this.

Then, last week,
the majority of us
voted against all of the above,
voted to restore the king,
voted for belief, in preference to knowledge,
voted against honesty,
voted against equality,
voted against inconvenient laws,
voted against truth,
voted against evidence,
voted against safety,
voted against health
voted against decency,
voted against their own best interests,
voted against thought itself,
voted against my country
and yes,
voted against me.

And for what:
the promises of a well known liar
for cheaper fuel to overheat the globe with,
more affordable ammunition,
higher football salary caps,
lower cost swine
and higher cost pearl.

The ideals
of myself
and others who grew up
never questioning
what was really good,
what was really bad
are now derided as some kind
of dad's joke,
steam powered,
wire wheeled
utopia of the woke
by the slumbering many.

Well,
how am I to cope with this:
move among those who support crime?
negotiate with those for whom truth is negotiable?
learn who, at any given moment, has privilege and who has not?
live from mean to mean to mean with no end in sight?
betray in order to avoid being a traitor?

Thanks, but no thanks.

While the emblems, ensigns, documents, mottos, songs and once
          victorious weapons
of my country
are being taken down

and stored away with the artifacts
of other empires that failed,
on e-bay
souvenirs of when there were elections
are being bartered
and shady shops that specialize in pornography
and banned books
offer The Grapes of Wrath
in a plain brown wrapper

Those of us
frightened for themselves and for their families
with no wish to experience life in camps
will, hopefully before it is too late,
seek other places
where, for now,
there is still some element of freedom,
some respect for justice,
some foundation of honest exchange
where thought and truth
are not vilified
and decency prevails.

So,
as in those old movie house travelogues,
while the sun gradually sets
we say farewell
to the United States of America
and its population
silhouetted
against the pyres of books,
burning in the park
busy moving
from lighthouse to lighthouse
making sure
they're dark.

What Time Do They Burn the Books?

As an author
I don't want to be late
they might burn my books without me
and one doesn't wish to miss
the major occasions
in one's life.

I mean,
for these people,
burning a book
is as close as they'll come to reading it
and the social aspects
are immense:
the communal execution of bound knowledge,
the sweating faces,
grinning
in the glow of the turning pages
Ah! The Nuremberg Rallies,
the Nazi mardi gras!
(Although, in retrospect,
it might have been wiser
to have celebrated in the winter.)

One thought troubles me,
however,
what if my books are not
chosen for the fire,
the biblio da fe.

What if what I have written
is deemed
insufficiently threatening
to the new order?
Shall I be,
like those unexecuted, untortured,
unimprisoned, unburnt Germans
of the 3rd reich
accused of complicity
with the attendant guilt
large enough to last
'til the next world war
and the regularly scheduled
expungement of the right?

Are
my slender little books
to sit on the sparsely populated shelves
next to the overweight, lightly thumbed volumes that are left
like Mein Kampf, The Art of the Deal,
The Secret History of the Mongols,
every Wisden, Foxe's Martyrs,
hymnals, motor manuals,
Kipling (shaking in his boots), telephone books of the Ukraine,
law statutes of disbanded countries,
row after dusty row in locked libraries
of books last borrowed
in the 20th century
quietly waiting for the next
pyre.

No,
it's not to be contemplated,
one must be careful
of the company one keeps
whether immediate
or extended
and these books, people,
even wearing dust jackets,
soil the neighbourhood.

So I think
I'll sneak some copies
of my stuff
into my pockets,
dance counter-clockwise
around the bonfire
humming Carmina Burana,
pretending
it's a pep rally
before the big game
and fling,
book by book,
my collected works
into the flames.

No chance then
of mistaking
what side I'm on.
It's the well done
one.

The Antique Roadshow

Any hussar who lives to 30 is a blackguard.
(General Antoine-Charles-Louis Lasalle, 1775-1809)

The roses are just right,
the bees untiring
in the gardens
of this stately building
built in someone's prime.

The lines of marked down people
in their op-shop clothes
flesh and hair
decaying at different ratios
holding onto their objects
that have dealt with time
more successfully than they.

Dogs,
making the best
of crawling,
are everywhere
their lack of curiosity
leading to endless
surprise.

The nattily dressed
staff,
their exhaustive research hidden
along with an urge
to patronize
which is definitely not permitted
though that is all there is here:
gardens, buildings, staff
and willing victims.

The anonymous TV camera
witnesses the judgements
on the wooden aeroplane propellor,
the x-chair
Machiavelli might have sat in,
the painting of a young woman
by a Victorian chap
known only to auctioneers,
a rare unopened canopic jar,
and a slightly used train set
from between the wars,
etc.

The pastichy theme plays
and all around the manicured grounds
the stately trees begin to drop their leaves
and the hereditary hosts their pretenses
'til only wiry, worn-out wigs
of twig and branch
ornament the set
where, as we speak, next years lines are starting to form
of the fading suitors who punched
well above their weight,
now, with no passion
left to unleash,
gingerly clutching
their slightly used pelisse,*
their fragile potiche.**

*pelisse: a fur lined jacket often worn over one shoulder by a
hussar, a light cavalryman.
**Potiche: an ornamental jar or vase that adorns many French
mantelpieces. Can be worth thousands or very little. Also
French slang for a "trophy wife".

This Here All Used to Be Fields

The vagaries of the aged,
the non sequiturs
may be simply
references to a world
the present generation
never lived in,
but is still
neighborhood to the old.

Drought

There's much to be said
for living with the weather
and sharing the seasonal
lives
of the bushes and herds.

But, just now,
when it's been
dry
for weeks
and the large semi-precious stones of
ponds
are cracked
into tesselated tan mosaics
on which
the communities of beasts
used to splash,

a world
shaded by a roof
at the end
of an aqueduct
has its attractions.

Because here
it's drought
all the way
to the waterline
where the surf
fries
when it meets the land
and beneath the sea's immense horizon
of contempt
people still drown
and sharks still prowl.

Early Winter, A.M.

I don't know anything about birds
but I like them,
as with women.
On this cold morning
one,
about the size of my hand,
is stepping,
wings folded back,
from branch to branch
limb to limb
stem to stem
some too slender
to bear its weight
but they keep their side of the agreement
and nothing breaks.
The black dots of eyes
dart,
the bright yellow beak
measures its balance
and its dance continues
shaking
a rain bangled spider web
like the cracked corner of a window,
rustling
the drying laundry of a leaf
until,
up to here with expertise
it says "to hell with it"
and flies
its wonderful wings
violently pushing the air aside,
showing
it's more than just a pretty face.

But,
she'll be back
(somehow I know it's a she)
to perform
the same polished movements
that is her job

just as my part of the agreement
is that I form an audience,
be an aficionado,
so quiet
that perhaps, finally,
she may mistake me
for a tree
and dance upon me.

For Michael Sharkey

Reading your
clever poems
I thought
wouldn't it be joy
to spend some hours together
exchanging epiphanies,
linking arms
with turns of phrase,
never being bored,
never losing the plot,
passing the point of it all
between us.

But,
it wouldn't work
you know
because I,
and maybe you,
wouldn't listen.
After offering my mot
to threaten your king

I'd turn away
hauling on the sheet
that raises my spinnaker
to embark on a new voyage
when you finally
finish
rattling on.

The Man in the Moon and Li Bo

Li Bo was an 8th century Chinese poet who was fond of drink and the moon,
whose reflection he tried to kiss only to fall in and drown.

Not
a very good likeness,
it's hard
to hold steady
with the sun full in your face
and still find
the water.

So, not my best work
but good enough
to make them all mad
and for
that old fool in China
to drink too much
and try to kiss me.

It makes one a bit giddy this
worship
from those with so little
wonder in their lives.
They lean out so far
to just touch
what is not even me:
only a nail cutting,
a glance,
a tear

and
lose their balance,
poor at the best of times,
falling
from the little nest of a home-made boat
onto the surface
of where they do not belong
plummeting
down,
deeper than light can stain
or colour make a livery,
thrashing in the liquefaction of their robes
to the untidy bottom of the sea
with all the other
thrown away, wasted debris.

My Father

After my father
had been on the wagon
for a couple of months
I asked him how it was going

"I'm so boring"
I thought he said.
"No, you're not" I replied.
Quickly interjecting he said
"No, no not me! Everybody else!"

He was the smartest person I ever knew,
solving, on the run,
problems in areas
he'd never entered before.

He drank too much,
he laughed too much,
he wept a bit,
he danced when he didn't know how to dance,
he was the life of every party.

Without education
he read Spinosa,
James Joyce,
Kissinger's books (so he could rebut them),
Paul Celan,
the Bhagavad Gita,
when I showed him poetry
he understood.

He never boasted
and he was undervalued
the whole of his moderately successful life
but he did
his work.

Getting home from the plant
to grab an avocado
from our tree,
open a beer
and picking a topic,
challenge his child
to choose a side and debate it.

He once told me a story
of when he and his great friend,
Walter Cope,
were roughnecks in the east Texas oilfields
and had been out on a bender
I see him in those old,
late hours,
his young, handsome face
sweating, listening,
hair mussed
as Walter suggested to him:
"Let's go see Mrs Hard
and get a good talking to."

Writing

From this ill assorted room,
items of furniture
disturbed from their spots,
dust motes falling
in the half light
I can look out over the papers
scattered on every surface

into the silent garden,
at its centre
the sunlit space of mown lawn,
around it the leaf brocaded scenery of the trees
and within the shade they produce
the tiffany lamps of flowers
as if waiting on small tables
to sit by.

I look at the quiet, benign
peace
of it
like a long awake man
looks at his bed,
yet,
when I open the door
and step into it
it is fled
like a reflection
trod upon.

Anastasia at the Dentist

When she asks you to change your appointment
her voice is like a consoling ointment

and when over her desk I hover
to find out what my insurance won't cover

I'm hardly bothered to see
that my excruciating pain is accompanied by a fee

and when she tells me, with consummate skill,
that the doctor has only just begun to drill

and though his ministrations are vicious
I'll soon have teeth totally fictitious

and when he dredges my root canal
her assurances that my discomfort is all banal

make me glad to find that she's not
the Anastasia who got shot.

For Isaac, on His 21st

It's a great distance
from there, 21
to 84, here.

If I had any wisdom
to utter
you wouldn't hear

and I don't blame you
since you're between beds
and I'm near my bier.

So go and do
some things I cannot do again
have a beer and a beer and a beer,

wink at a pretty girl
you do not know,
make a quick movement without fear,

wander in an open door
confident that welcome
and smiles will appear,

know what's in, what's out,
enter and run the race
sure you won't be in the rear,

and if you make a mistake or two
simply resort to that saline solution,
a tear.

I Died in 2023

I died in 2023
and I thought that would be it
but it isn't
it's moving around
through old photograph albums,
nearly all posed,
very few snaps.
Surprising, how that disappoints,
the failure to take advantage
of the awesome inventions
and ambush life
and its wonderful accidents
and, of course, the people you run into
are all dead,
the lack of colour
goes unnoticed.
I can even write these words
which is, perhaps, afterlife
for poets
messages hammered and coaxed out
collected into books:
gatherings of bird formations
on a given hour
of a given day
that no one reads
but most, praise.

So, sitting in a train station
with these time tables of my past
on the walls
I find someone else's newspaper
on the bench
dated 2025
and I quickly turn to the sports section
to see how my teams did
bemused to learn how little
another loss means
and, fearfully, to the front page
to find my country
has elected someone eminently unsuited
to be their dictator

and that the bad news
has become the good news
and that I am the future.

Dementia

Him:
It's like
living in a library
filled with books you read once
but can't remember
and,
because you don't read anymore,
books
you've never read

all somebody else's world
while you,
your mind increasingly shortsighted,
can only keep adjusting your focus inward
waiting
for your order
to be filled
among
fluctuating
strangers.

Me:
For years
he was my mate
but we parted badly
and now
he's not my,
nor anyone's, mate
but his own
anymore.

I read his books,
hung his paintings
on my walls
wanting
his reality to be part
of my building.

He threw
the incomparable wit
of his conversation
out, out
over and over
like an ornate boomerang and,
I suppose,
one day it didn't come back.

Around me
the population enlarges,
new generations
in their thousands
trying to fix the same machines
we did
surge and spill,
but there are a number
of largely
inaccessible and vacant spaces
where they can't go
or I, obstinately,
won't let them
fill.

Mrs. McKellar

For Kathleen Jamie

Mrs. McKellar who lives next door
can't decide
to be on the telly
or be a whore.

Mrs. McKellar in number nine
watching the traffic
and saving her twine.

Mrs. McKellar of the shabby fence
whose cat we torment
for her difference.

Mrs. McKellar and her unseen inside
the presence of a husband
neither confirmed or denied.

Mrs. McKellar walks toward the railway track
and a faint suspicion
that she'll never be back.

And when Mrs. McKellar's cord is finally cut
some will grieve, but more will wonder
if the coffin's to be open or shut.

Joe Biden

Violins
made in the 16th century
are still in use and demand
but not the violinists.
We wear out
and whether from playing good or bad music
seems to make no difference.

A point in every life
is reached
when utility is lost,
although,
it is a requisite of life itself
that this use-by-date
must be ignored
until too late.

So Joe Biden,
an entire life already lived,
intervened to defend us,
once more,
from the worst of the suppurating world
and from the worst of ourselves.
Another victory
and now
another tragedy.

So, no more
long, perilous stairways
from Air Force One,
just the chosen
level paths
from one safe place to another
and no more
the edited and reedited
and pounded flat speeches
to the vast anonymous
millions
who may listen,
replaced
by a hand on elbow
or shoulder
or back
an exchanged message
between faces of concern
and no more gratitude
you can't trust,
no more hatred
you can't question
no more Easter egg hunts
in smallish rooms
for truth
so artfully hidden,
no more having to ignore
those who love you
for those
whose names now escape you.

Perhaps,
it's time for the garden
and plants who don't complain,
just bloom or die
whatever seems right

and, finally,
maybe a burial at sea:
the body wrapped and muted,
slips from under
the flag of his country,
a small deposit,
into an ocean
too vast to either be cleansed or
polluted.

Supreme Court

Past the white corduroy columns
between the impossibly ornate doors
through the guided tours
the plaintiffs,
witnesses,
lawyers
there for their last chance
further on
earnest young justices-to-be
with important looking documents
come out under
costly name plates
giving glimpses
of opulent chambers
and other earnest persons
all wearing similar suits
that don't clash
with the building.

Eventually
you meet less expensive
uniforms
and finally an unornate set of doors
opens onto the unairconditioned world.
Streets
with darned pot holes
where every person has a flaw
each a piece from a different game

and nothing in the neighbourhood
matches
and important things
are carried by everyone
as they move past the trees that live there too
each deciding
when to compromise
with the weather
and give up their leaves

and all of the improvised,
discordant buildings
do not bother to ring hollow,
the lights
don't reflect from the burnished floors
and the men and women in them
get lost
because of the endless complexity
of acts that both violate and obey
the many letters of the law.

Unlike
those who wander off course
because of the self-induced,
finite simplicity
found in marble monoliths,
earnestly belabouring the obvious
into the obscure
exchanging value for cost

never once noticing
that they're lost.

Rank and File

When I was in the army
we draftees used to speak,
in a contemptuous way,
about R.A.s, i.e. regular army,
and others who liked
the military life
as someone
who had "found a home".

A feng shui home
filled with tradition,
ritual,
rules,
customs,
folded beds
like freshly made sandwiches,
and everything else
that could be trained for
and instinct,
talent
are pejoratives.

Since,
in such a life of tiny tolerances,
mistake
is all but certain,
there were many
who did not like it
including
criminals,
geniuses
and most of the members
of that large subversive group
recognizable
by bad complexions,
worse taste
and a general misunderstanding of the past
known in some circles
as youth
and
all the others unable to resist
their sense of humour.

Anatevka*, after the Jews

They handled it pretty well,
the children,
the old people,
the bundled goods
on the carts
drawn by the men
acting as draught animals

oh, some tears
here and there
and some looks,
at me,
like bills run up
and owing,
as if it were my
fault.

But,
on the whole,
it was well managed,
you could tell they'd
done this before,
an experienced circus
that moved in a column
down the road from the village
to the left turning
disappearing
to their next engagement.

And now,
any crowd is quieter
and what music there is
a bit off (they could do gypsy better than us),
it's hard to get a decent seam
sewn,
or a good deal,
or an argument that goes up at the end

but little has changed,
little ever changes

After the sticky beaks looked
in the buildings
they left behind
and found them
not so different
from ours
we settled in:
their cows give the same
amount of milk,
their chickens lay the same number
of eggs,
oval as toys.

At least,
no more pogroms,
no more Sundays
in a church full of accomplices to a crime still in commission.

No,
the bad mood of the weather
they left behind,
the frozen mud,
like carven despair, they left
behind
and Him,
that dark magistrate
of a God,
they left behind.

*Anatevka: The turn of the century Russian village where
  Sholom Aleichem's "Fiddler on the Roof" takes place.

Mise en Scene

As if ducking
to avoid the night,
the earth tips
and morning light
spills into my back garden
and the pale tracery of bare branches
gradually show up against the dark
like slow lightning,
and the action
begins again
from where it left off
when night came.

The hue and cry
of birds crossing
from stage left
between the furniture of plants
and leaves move
as the trees shake themselves awake.
I have a good seat
as I settle down
to watch the play
play out.

Schadenfreude

A decorated officer of the crown,
an honoured historian
whose histories were official
had been
drinking
all afternoon with his mates
when we arrived
to have dinner
with he and his imposing wife.
His taxi coming simultaneously
to stop beside us
he invited the driver
to dine with us.
The driver declined and drove away,
taking with him any possibility
that the merriment of the afternoon
would continue.

I
helped him carry bags of groceries
including a couple of packages of kippers
which he had somehow confused
with the smoked salmon
noted on the shopping list.

His wife's vocal dismay
only caused his face,
already creased by grog,
to bend slightly
Helen and I bit down on our expressions.

Pre-dinner drinks
were poured into glasses
that his wife hoped had an apparent history
of expenditure.
During this part of the presentation
he tried,
beguilingly,
to lure the family dog to sit beside him,
it would not leave his wife's feet.
Another little bend.

The kippers ignored,
we went straight into the roasting
on a newly acquired Weber.
He returned to manage to sit,
with a distinct list,
at a small electric piano
and with a smile and gesture
reminiscent of making a leg
and sweeping the ground with a feathered hat
he hoped that I, as an American,
would like his arrangement of Gershwin.
I realized
I could not stop him.

When he reached the climax
of his celebration of Gershwin
it had not been
a smooth journey,
there had been many missteps
on the rope bridge of the keyboard,
false starts,
repeats,
bits not quite remembered right.

But he swivelled
an enormous grin
clearly feeling the great composer's arm around his shoulders,
his wife sniffed,
(the dog had left in the middle)
and we hurriedly arranged our faces
into ramshackled delight.

Another bend.

He then went, with rather fierce prompting from stage left,
to bring in the main course.
Being new to the Weber
he had not closed or left open the lid (I forget which)
and the meat looked like something
that had suffered while re-entering
earth's atmosphere
and he carried it in,
a small, black asteroid
that we pretended to eat.

When we reached the car
we couldn't wait to look at each other,
our smirks turning into guffaws
anticipating dining out on that evening
for years to come.

A few months later he died
when his heart attacked him.
Schadenfreude
means the enjoyment
of the pain of others

I hope, Ian,
you are enjoying mine.

Vicki Viidikas

They're writing a book about Vicki.
I suppose they will write a book about everybody,
all of them missing the point.

When I first met her
to buy her papers
I knew her name
but not her writings,
her reputation
but not what had earned it.

The face creased
like something put away wrong,
the seductiveness
like a plate of canapes
served in the middle of the dessert course.

Later, amid the detritus of her life,
in the scrapbooks
I saw the photographs
of the sunlit, beautiful girl,
read the impetuous, agile words
and felt pity for what she had come to

and, comparing her state with mine,
wondered if she had a choice,
I know I did,
and whether it was the right one.

But the year can't be judged by the Christmas dinner
or a life by the funeral.
Perhaps further back
pushing into a time crowded like a piss-up in a cheap flat
filled with options and party crashers
and music the same age as you
is where worth will be found.

The books about Vicki
have already been written
by an expert
with access to all the necessary information,
every successful image,
overwhelming emotion,
the only things she left out
were trivia and typos.

After You Left

After you left
I finally decided
to change the pictures
in the house
and when I took yours down
it left a pale space
on the wall
and it reminded me
of the untanned lines
left by your bathing suit

and I thought
of how It felt
to slowly pull the strap
aside.

War

The raised voice,
the fierce, tightened look,
the trespass of personal space,
the quick push,
the fear,
the drunken question
(with no query, no answer),
that question repeated,
the intervention by onlookers,
the hope for allies,
maybe lawyers,
but anyway, more official,
the formal clothes,
that makes it less personal,
and acquisition of precedents,
people who agree with you,
the friends who no longer speak,
the organizing,
the research,
the larger venue,
neither side
negotiating in good faith,
justifying the elongation of peace
by looking for better weapons,
the ultimatums,
the vague realization that most damage is collateral,
finally,
War,
when the bar fight
can no longer be avoided,
destruction,
including the tavern this started in,
and all the death
that nobody wanted.

For Stella's Birthday
For Stella Tome

That last birthday at home
seems
like a beginning
but it isn't
it's an ending
and every one after that
tells you
how far away you've come

and the ones that happen
in a foreign place
are even farther
like those birds
who, miles out to sea,
can land on a wave
and watch, with calm curiosity,
your boat go by.

The token gifts, choreographed
meals, vague, half obsequies
are polite attempts
to obscure
the inevitable occurrence
of the next one.

On Not Having a Mobile Phone

In my phone book
are numbers
of my parents
and ex-wives,
dentists from when I had teeth,
friends who haven't called in a while
and friends
I can't quite remember
but liked enough
to make an inscription
of how to reach them,
some addresses
on streets now renamed,
some countries
overrun

and if I discard
that molded hand
of a telephone
and the number it's always had
won't I miss them
when they call
again?

Things Written for Children
and Geoff Page's Birthdays

Atticus

For Atticus Lupa Menardo

So here's the reason for all the fuss:
A young gentleman named Atticus
Who's been Geli's personal Anschluss,
Who caused Elizabeth to miss her bus,
And Tom to leave the Age of Aquarius.

Who's come to wrinkle and come to muss:
Be our own boots 'n' puss,
A polymath, an intellectual platypus
So hitch up your 3 sided truss
And receive a welcome from all of us

Who've been here so long we're more minus than plus
Come and be our new amanuensius.

For Jessica

for Jessica Brooks

I have, inadvertently, taken your horse,
it's the pink one that goes well with a blue race course
and I have, inadvertently, taken your horse.

It appeared this evening in the pocket of my coat,
at first, I thought it was merely an undressed goat
but its mane and its tail and hooves caused me to say, and I quote,
That I have, inadvertently, taken your horse.

Here I am, as the day is just starting to bustle,
exercising every embarrassment muscle
because I have committed an accidental rustle
and I have, inadvertently, taken your horse.

I can imagine the gasps of alarm
at the cavernous gap in the barn
the cries of alas, alack and oh darn!
for I have, inadvertently, taken your horse.

I hope you are not given to pouts
just because discourteous louts
make off with your favourite mounts
for I have, inadvertently, taken your horse.

But hark! a thought has just caused my depression to shift
and given my feelings a lift
perhaps it was not theft, but a gift!
and I have Not, inadvertently, taken your horse.

For Stella

Someone's nana gave me a card
that someone had worked on very hard.

It is purple with red and yellow hearts
carefully folded into two parts.

When opened, I found it was addressed to me,
but who it was from was not so easy to see.

It was written in red like an elegant logo
and signed by someone named Stella Xoxo.

Who, I wondered, could Miss Xoxo be?
Did she live in a caravan parked by the sea?

And then I thought, "Stella" means star
but a card by hand couldn't have come far.

So, someone nearby who twinkles,
probably with a voice that tinkles

and maybe a mother named Kate
who has an Ant for a mate

and a Leo for a brother.
No, it couldn't be any other!

Now I know the Stella who sent this card
that was worked on so very, very hard.

This card worth more than money can buy
Came from Stella, the only Stella

for she's a Jolly Good Stella
and so say all of I!

The Day Geoff Page Wore an Hawaiian Shirt

Geoff is well known for dressing only in shades of brown, beige, white and gray.

In Canberra, where day bends but never breaks
and where bridges precede the lake,

the concrete walls reflect themselves in the dawn
and the day widens into a stubbled yawn.

An average morning, gray and leaden,
with no warning of the impending Armageddon,

Geoff, after a sleepless night considering the shirt, decided to wear it.
At one stroke, changing from pigeon to parrot.

The shirt, on one side featured a crimson Zulu,
on the other, a purple map of Honolulu.

It was made of machine stitched, yellow rayon, shiny and viscous
and on each sleeve, an embroidered hibiscus.

Altogether, the kind of sartorial hubbub
only ever seen at the odd league's club.

As he emerged that morning, like a cocktail Molotov,
his ambient light was enough to turn the street lights off

and the pale scholars of ecole Narrabundah
had never in their lives seen such a wundah.

Classes were cancelled and tea ladies fainted,
There were walls on which graffiti was painted.

A principal, with the demeanour of Bulldog Drummond,
requested that the authorities be summoned

and generally, there was the feeling that an era had passed.
Someone, thoughtfully, lowered the flag to half-mast.

Finally, Geoff had to assess what he had done,
whether more respect was lost or won,

for there's no going back to the shades of wonton,
as Villon almost said·."mais ou sont les beige d'antan?"

.

3 Score 10 Meets Geoff Page

Every 10 years or so
I give light verse a go
Because Mister Page
Has added 10 more years of age.

I'm even older than Geoff
So who knows how much is left
And the mental sinews aren't so supple,
This year I thought I'd better write a couple.

But, please, don't take fright
I don't intend to read them both tonight.
No, just the one about seventy
Attempting to treat decay with levity.

The theme about which I'll wax sage
Is the instruction I received "not to mention beige",
For my last go at doggerelled mirth
Fantasized on Geoff wearing a Hawaiian shirt.

So this time no blanc mange verse
But, probably something, rather, worse.
Perhaps a sheepskin of flattery
Removed too soon from the tannery;

Reams of endless malarkey
Bound uniformly in khaki;
A somewhat used laurel wreath
Stained to the colour of 70 year old teeth;

A cluster of comments that ought to be bright
Managing just to achieve a sort of off-white;
The master potter at his wheel
Running his fingers through the oatmeal;

Of course, there's always hope:
That withered limb sheathed in taupe.
"Where is he going? I hear you murmur
"he's down on his knees searching the berber."

Well, I've found what I want to say about age,
It's not so tough, it doesn't work on Geoff Page
. . . . and I hardly mentioned Beige.

We Clever Fellows

We clever fellows
come along
and punch the enormous, cushioned mystery
bouncing,
harmlessly,
off its insolubility

since
what lies beyond our eulogies
can't be known
it is this celestial
shock absorber
that makes us sentient ones
continue
to play the game

and because the dice
we throw
have more spots than
the stars
no one finally loses,
no one is finally
wrong
or
right.

About us,
breathing
its gigantic breaths
the universe exhales
and inhales:
the bellows
of infinity

Oh, I'm close,
so close,
nearer than I've ever been
to the incandescent
joy
of knowing

aware
there's no knowing
to be known
that ignorance
is the sentinel of bliss
and that the game,
whose box and instructions
were lost long ago,
is still afoot.

Memo

I have always had a knack
for finding things
probably,
because I am often lost
and because
of a Holden Caufield
kind of sense of empathy
with the regret
of those
for whom something important
or necessary
is missing from their lives
and I want
so much
to restore them
to what they were,
avoiding
the time spent
in searching
and the missed appointments
and neglected opportunities.

It began
with my grandmother,
then my parents.
I knew them so well
all their bits and pieces,
where they should be
where they might be
working backward
through their many habits
to the miscreant
thing

replacing the loosened gem
that has rolled away
returning it
for the respect
for my omniscience

and after my family
I found things
for my bosses,
my lovers,
my wives
time increasing
my little business

Until, I start the day
checking
for the presence
of the familiar
counting off
my remaining faculties
wondering
where I left
my keys.

Love vs Thought

What can one creature among other creatures do but love?
Carlos Drummond de Andrade (tr. Richard Zenith)

I hate to disagree with someone I like
but you are wrong, Carlos,
thought,
not love,
is what we humans must do.

Love,
like hope that has gone off,
is the animals' solution
and we have left that behind.

The beasts
do not sense the mystery
and only see it
as the unease
we bring into their lives.
Their loves
stop at speciate borders,
their arguments
are all the same

while we,
who place numbers on our lairs
so strangers may find us,
can only think our way
through
or hide
from the awesome multiplication
that thought brings

Garry Shead

and when the way is not clear,
and it never is,
and even maps
do not know the way
we think a new atlas
for who has not walked the streets
and seen the clutter
that gives the lie
to the immaculate maps

which only work
if you know where you are going

and we do not,
and we do not,
and we do not,

Yet, let us hope it is somewhere interesting
where our destination lies
and not the answers
without questions
of a bought off the plan paradise.

The Professional Mourner

I have dabbled in mourning
most of my life
just when I'm sure
something or someone is solid,
load bearing
they,
it
slip away,
another bit to which
I didn't realize
I had to hold,
leaving the structure
to be shored,
façade touched up

and there is
another corner stone
to find
a new true north to divine
until
after the years
my compass is hopelessly
confused
and I
am the only direction left.

Garry Shead

As the last
funeral rite approaches
it is wearying
to be so unsure
of how sad to be,
so I will dress
in inky black,
tearing the clothes
made to be torn,
make a loud lamentation,
join the slow procession
behind the blacked-up horses
in black bondage
spikes of black plumes jutting from their heads,
ebony unicorns stepping carefully,
only the dung is technicolor,
and I will become
a Professional Mourner,
accepting that all before
has only been a hiatus
and finally lose
my amateur status.

The Emperor's Tailor

For Kate Pearcy

It started
a while ago
when I was new
to the trade
and he,
simply a prince
of a principality
known only to cartographers.

But,
he needed his clothes,
his uniforms
from defeated armies
and sunken navies

and so I made him garments
as out of style
as he was,
more an archeologist
than a tailor,

and he really couldn't pay
what they cost.

Then he inherited an empire
that didn't exist
with valuable dust
on all the antiques
and
infinitely more expensive attire

and I said,
pushing back my eye shade,
"what if I just tell you about the imperial wardrobe,
what you're wearing,
what it looks like
rather than endlessly
stitching all that braid?"

and he
giggled.

His entourage,
living in their parents',
parents', parents' houses
with furniture
one daren't sit on,

who couldn't afford
to notice,
lest their profound
expertise
in nothing
be exposed,

praised the boss's new clothes
as "subtle,
understated,
with no profane
clutching at reality"

meaning:
too subtle to be interrogated;
too oblique to be defined;
too accommodating to be satirized.

So,
on I go
from one season to the same season
with greatly reduced overheads and
on the infrequent
openings of my door
a breeze disturbs the rack
of dusty coat hangers
that rock like little planes
lining up to land on their carrier.
But,
I did win a Derrida
for Conspicuous Deconstruction,
there was that article in Vogue
and, evidently, I've influenced others
in the small world of tailoring
plus,
I do get to put that sign
outside:
"Tailor, By Appointment to His
Imperial Majesty"

oh,
you didn't see it?

New Poems

Annoying the Pig

Never try to teach a pig to sing. It wastes your time and it annoys the pig.
Robert Heinlein

Maybe it's useless
to continue to argue
with those
whose minds are blunt instruments,

their history of utterances
so limited in vocabulary
as to be close on
illiterate,
blunder after blunder
based
on the first mistake
that comes along,

so frightened
by the uncertainty of life
that their sole solution
is the reduction of options
to single digits.

But yet,
though the urge is to migrate
from this eyeless kingdom of the blind,
I feel a duty
to re-engage
and not neglect the obligation
that surely rests
with all people of decency
to try to preserve liberty
for those
who can make some
use of it.

Poets

For Eleanor Sharwood

We poets
write poetry,
but our lives
are prose.

The poems
are considered,
reconsidered,
polished
and rearranged.

Set out
and offered
in the best light
we can find
to attract
just the reaction
we hope for.

It is our craft,
what we're good at
but
in our lives
we're careless amateurs
lost
with no maps or charts,
asking directions
from strangers in the street

as lost
as we,
a work that happens to us,
unshaped,
with no dramatic pauses
only awkward silences
where we are left without words
stumbling
into an unplanned,
unclever
ending.

And everybody
knows that story,
so, who wants to read about that?
when it could be
surprising,
special,
catchy as pain,
sad as absence,
amusing as a laugh escaping,
something very like that first time,
a sentence that doesn't stop
with a period
but a rhyme.

Building the Bunker

For Duncan and Laurie Gray

Sometime ago
I left the film set saloon
of life
gun drawn,
backing out
through the swinging doors
into retirement.

Holed up
in my old house,
walls
thick as my skin,
with years
of sophisticated mysteries
cored around unlikely crimes
that, admittedly,
I have always known
will be solved
while, outside,
cowboys
hoorahed the town.

As it became
more and more hazardous
to go out
I stayed behind the door
turning my back on the street

and turning my back yard
into a clearing
in the forest
green as a pool table
fringed with flowers
the colour of billiard balls.

In the interior of the interior
a bunker
of what civilization
used to be,
reading lamp lit,
art from the last dynasty
on the walls,
music from when melody
and wit
knew each other
plays,
I sit with Sondheim, Lester,
Yeats, Shead, Wallace-Crabbe,
Vivaldi
and many other of the unsane,
complicit
in their resistance
to the simple, obvious,
ordinary, erosive
religion
of the mundane.

At the same time
in another part of the town
young men
leave their windows open
polluting the boulevards
with their songs,
busy creating
what a preceding age
discarded
calling it new and unsold,
confusing different
with good,

meeting
in the evenings
at the wine bars
with friends
who congratulate
each other
on not being old.

www.ingramcontent.com/pod-product-compliance
Lightning Source LLC
Chambersburg PA
CBHW050014090426
42734CB00020B/3269